Dedicated to
Mi Madre

"I came from an era when you had to be nice to men. I remember my mom saying that to me. She said, 'You be a nice girl and if a man tells you to do this or that, you do it. OK?' And let me tell you, that has its effect. It's lasting. It took me a very, very, very long time to feel independent."

—Rita Moreno

Associated Press interview, published in the *San Francisco Chronicle*, February 25, 2019.

Leticia Aguilar And
Eve Quesnel

LEAVING PATRIARCHY BEHIND

One Woman's Journey

AUSTIN MACAULEY PUBLISHERS™

LONDON • CAMBRIDGE • NEW YORK • SHARJAH

Ordering Information
Quantity sales: Special discounts are available on quantity purchases by corporations, associations, and others. For details, contact the publisher at the address below.

Publisher's Cataloging-in-Publication data
Aguilar, Leticia and Quesnel, Eve
Leaving Patriarchy Behind

ISBN 9781638295945 (Paperback)
ISBN 9781638295969 (ePub e-book)
ISBN 9781638295952 (Audiobook)

Library of Congress Control Number: 2022920689

www.austinmacauley.com/us

First Published 2023
Austin Macauley Publishers LLC
40 Wall Street,33rd Floor, Suite 3302
New York, NY 10005
USA

mail-usa@austinmacauley.com
+1 (646) 5125767

We would like to thank:

Amy Anderson, who transcribed pages and pages of audio recordings. Her professionalism and swift responses greatly helped move this project along. Thanks as well to Voice Record Pro for its ease and dependable recording, alongside Rev.com for its fast and efficient transcripts. Many thanks to Monina Vázquez and Ali Urza for translating the interview with Leticia's mother. Devon LaBonte and Austin Macauley Publishers—they saw the 'poignancy' in this work and took a chance on us. At AMP, Jennifer Lane, our production coordinator, answered all our questions and kept us organized and moving forward. Thank you, Jennifer!

I [Leticia] would like to thank Eve, my college instructor, who, after hearing my story at an event, made a promise to get my story out into the world. Shane McConkey encouraged me to tell my story. He seemed to understand the trials of Mexican women. I might never have enrolled in college had it not been for Ruth Hall. She understood the influence I could have on the Latinx community, and so encouraged my education and membership in the Family Resource Center and Soroptimist Organization. My son, Juan, was my constant support, telling me never to give up. My husband, Romero, took care of things at home while I worked on this project.

I [Eve] would like to thank, foremost, Leticia, for her bravery in telling her story and for inspiring women to gain the independence they so desperately crave. Candy Blesse has heard Leticia's story from the beginning—now ten years in—and been supportive during the joyous times as well as the challenging ones. Suzanne Roberts, professionally and as a good friend, is always available for advice and assistance, no matter what stage of a project. Ann Ronald, Mike Branch, Cheryl Glotfelty, Tracy Wager, Jans Wager, and Kim Bateman, I thank them for their willingness to help at any turn. To the Surprise Valley Writers' Conference and to Ray and Barbara March, the motivating force behind many aspiring authors, a heartfelt thank you. From the SVWC, many thanks to Max Byrd, Jessica Hughes, Terry Miller, Caleb Leisure, and Logan Seidl for their thoughtful feedback, Kandi Maxwell, too. I acknowledge Ana Maria Spagna for reminding me 'to touch the trail,' Chris Coake for advocating the importance of 'the trouble,' and Janisse Ray for promoting the senses. The writing posse I met up on the hill—Christina Nemec, David Bunker, Derek Larson, and Jude Goodpaster—they always asked the right questions. Laurel Lippert, my breakfast writing companion, her meticulous editing made this book that much better. Jim Porter, his legal advice steered us toward a more fruitful direction. Leticia's family in Mexico, I thank them for their grace, their kindness, and their hospitality when I visited Leticia's hometown, Vista Hermosa. I would like to recognize my mother, Marlo Erickson, who encourages me to keep writing. Lastly, a heartfelt thank you to my husband, Quiz, and daughter Kim. I never take their love and support for granted.

Table of Contents

Foreword   **11**

Introduction Sugarcane Village   **14**

List of Children   **19**

Yesterday 1   **21**

Chapter 1: Babies   23

Chapter 2: Tomato Hair   26

Chapter 3: Period   28

Chapter 4: Ten Minutes Before Ten   30

Chapter 5: Pesos   32

Chapter 6: Punishment   34

Chapter 7: Raul   36

Chapter 8: The Decision   39

Chapter 9: Three Days and Three Nights   43

Chapter 10: Crossings   48

Chapter 11: A False Marriage   52

Chapter 12: United States   54

Yesterday 2   **57**

Chapter 13: Boyfriends   59

Chapter 14: Marriage   63

Chapter 15: Gaby   67

Chapter 16: They Call Me Tecia   70

Chapter 17: José Parra in Jail   73

Chapter 18: Papa's Last Words   75

Chapter 19: Money   79

Chapter 20: Reaching for Raul   81

Chapter 21: College   85

Chapter 22: Interview with Mama   88

Chapter 23: Mama's Last Words   92

Today   **97**

Chapter 24: Jesus in a Glass House, Guadalupe
    in Every House   99

Chapter 25: Jealous   103

Chapter 26: Small Steps   106

Tomorrow   **109**

Chapter 27: Ramiro Changing   111

Chapter 28: Skin Deep   114

Epilogue: Tomatoes   118

Foreword

I first met Leticia in the spring of 2007 in a community college classroom. We were close in age—only one year apart—both having just entered our fiftieth decade. I was teaching a course titled "Critical Thinking and Writing about Literature." In the class, we examined collected works in a variety of genres while considering themes, components of literature, and writing styles. As I was reading Leticia's responses to the assigned pieces, I came to know her *own* stories, growing up in a small town in Mexico and then immigrating to the United States.

In October 2011, I attended a Soroptimist reception in our hometown Truckee, California, to honor and celebrate Leticia. That year she was named the 2011 Woman of Distinction, chosen for her community work in bridging the Caucasian and Latino communities, and in aiding women in achieving their goals. One year later, in 2012, Leticia received the Rotary Club Citizen of the Year award.

At the Soroptimist reception, Leticia recounted her life in summary, captivating a packed recreation hall. After her presentation, I found myself in a circle of women where I heard one woman say, "Someone should write Leticia's story." It was clear from the beginning of the evening, as Leticia described her history and presented her beliefs, that her narrative needed to be told.

Soon after the award-winning event, Leticia visited my home where I set a pad of paper filled with questions, and a tape recorder, on my living room table. To my surprise, week after week the list was ignored as each time Leticia entered my house she'd say, "I know what I'd like to talk about today." I quickly learned, Leticia was quite a storyteller.

Four months after I began interviewing Leticia I traveled to Vista Hermosa, Mexico, the small village of her birth and childhood. At the village, I met her mother (who is no longer alive) whom I videotaped while Leticia asked her questions in Spanish. I couldn't help but be in awe of the diminutive elderly woman, dressed in her finest gray suit, a woman who, in an impoverished setting, had given birth to eighteen children and raised fifteen.

From the beginning, Leticia knew she was different from the rest of her family, knew it wasn't only necessary but imperative to turn a dysfunctional environment, no matter how tied to custom, into one that granted fairness and equality. Leticia defied the patriarchal society she was born into and achieved feats even she could never have imagined.

Leticia moved to America at fourteen years old as a caregiver to one of her older sister's five children in Sacramento, California. There, when time allowed, she learned English by sitting in the back of her nieces' and nephews' classrooms four to five times a week. While in Sacramento, from the ages of sixteen to seventeen, Leticia picked tomatoes in the fields and worked at a laundry. At twenty, she took her GED exam in Mexico, and at age twenty-two married a man from her hometown who worked back in the United States at a lumber mill. In the community

12

of Truckee, surrounded by pines and firs in the Sierra Nevada mountains, Leticia became a wife, a mother, a grandmother, obtained two Associate degrees, and started her own successful business.

The following vignettes illustrate Leticia's life as she remembers them. The topics and words are a compilation of both our efforts.

Eve Quesnel

Introduction
Sugarcane Village

After a two-hour drive from the bustling city of Guadalajara, the town of Santa Cruz—later named Vista Hermosa—abruptly announces itself with a sudden burst of greenery, hundreds of acres of sugarcane, eight-foot-tall sentinels lined up in rows, declaring a thriving economy, a means by which an entire town makes a living.

Beginning with tilling and planting, then cutting and burning, the workers take a brief respite before gathering the charred sugarcane, the perennial grass crop that permeates the air with a sweet, burnt smell. The workers, dark-skinned from working day after day in the hot sun, load the large bundles of sugarcane onto a row of trucks that are driven to the factory on the hill, much like a string of elephants, tails attached to one another. A year later, the process begins anew as billows of black smoke rise above the lush green valley.

Vista Hermosa and three other villages nearby bring sugar to the world, small granular beads that people dip spoons and measuring cups into and mix with flour, butter, and baking powder to create delectable desserts. They bring the sweet that infuses the world's body.

Above the sugarcane fields, the small village climbs to the top of the gently rising hills, each "block" a long wall of concrete, each "house" separated from the next by a mere door or iron gate that leads into a small garden or narrow hallway. From this outside corridor, a side door leads to the actual residence.

The homes are as much outside as inside, courtyards built as adjacent rooms, lively with copper pots steaming over open fires set on brick foundations. Laundry hangs near the fires with men's soiled white undershirts and children's faded dresses. Sometimes a dog paces in the yard, anxiously waiting for a scrap of food to be tossed its way; other times it lies outside the front door or gate on the dirt street, to welcome all who visit.

Across the street from a young girl named Leticia, a close family friend, Lupé, makes her living by selling tortillas, aided by her daughter. Every day they begin in the courtyard, their small family-run business; every night they go to bed, their hands callused from the many years the daughter has stirred the masa, kneaded the dough, placed the small balls into the press, pushed down the handle with her weight, and tossed the hand-sized circles of cornmeal onto a cast iron grill. Lupé, following after her daughter, picks up the tortillas off the hot grill with a swift pinch of her fingers and rolls the small tortillas with a hefty rolling pin, to stretch their hides. The tortillas, stacked like pancakes, thirty high, pronounce another job well done, another day of making a living from the corn, the yellow grain once hidden in rows of green, much like the sugarcane.

The sugarcane factory, Inhenyo de Vista Hermosa, stands proudly on a hill at the corner of the village like a general keeping watch over his rows of soldiers below. Gray concrete, three stories high, a church with a bell tower

15

at its rear, the factory stretches from one of the lower corners of the town square to the upper corner, an entire block long. The lower corner houses the owner and his family, one side boasting big, bold rooms decorated with large, heavy pieces of furniture—wooden tables, beds, and dressers embellished with chunky wood carvings of flowers and birds. The dining room shows off a glittery gold chandelier with tapered candles reaching toward the high white-washed ceiling. On each wall in each room, the Virgin Mary, Guadalupe—a delicate brushstroke of white thin lines emanating from her head—watches over the factory owner and his family.

The sugarcane family sleeps soundly in the grand, impressive rooms while the workers walk to work from their humble homes across the street or up the hill, after having been awakened by the crow of many roosters. When they arrive to start their shifts, the owner rustles out of bed to enjoy papayas and bananas and scurries his children off to school. Soon after, he walks to the other end of the factory to talk to the foreman to lay out the schedule, payments, and other activities of the day. As the morning begins to stir, the factory begins to hum.

One worker, José Garcia Parra, a tall handsome man with bushy eyebrows and dark, thick hair, heads to the noise-filled factory—the machines shredding and crushing the sugarcane—in his gray coveralls and heavy boots. To begin, he hands out chains for tying down the sugarcane piled high on overfilled trucks. After, he documents the name of each driver and the number of chains he distributed. Finally, he records the weight of each truck. The owners are good to José Parra; they know he is smart, can read and write, is honest and responsible; they make him a supervisor. When two of his sons, Pepé and Ruben, are old enough, fifteen, they too march off to the sugarcane factory to work a long day and sometimes into the early evening.

Before he leaves his house, José Parra grabs his lunch, quickly made by his petit and demure wife, Maria, who shortly after his departure settles into the routine of taking care of her brood—ten, twelve, fifteen, however many children remain while others grow older and move out on their own.

Leticia, one of the youngest, the rambunctious tomboy and often troublemaker in the family, watches her mother scurry about, cooking, cleaning, washing clothes outside in the courtyard. On any day, she might help her attach the clothes to the clothesline where they hang listlessly until a rare breeze comes along, giving the row of newborn to teenager-sized clothes movement and life. Another day, she might aid in the daily chores by sitting on a stool, stirring a hot posole, thick with pinto beans and hominy.

Maria had given birth to Leticia in their humble home; the other children were born there, too, except for the two babies when Maria was ill and enlisted the help of doctors in the bigger hospital outside of town.

Leticia remembers one time, directly after one of her brothers or sisters was born—she can't recall which one—her mama stumbled toward the kitchen while bleeding onto the floor. This is the only time Leticia can picture her mother crying. Her father sat sullenly at the table, waiting for his tortillas and beans and sliced mangos to be rolled together in brown paper so that he could go to work.

In this way, the rhythm of Vista Hermosa sang. The birthing of babies. The rolling of tortillas. The burning of the fields. The preparing of lunches.

In this way, Leticia looks back at her life.

Eve Quesnel

List of Children

Mother: Maria Gonzalez Villa, August 15, 1921 – December 22, 2016
Father: José Garcia Parra, March 9, 1917 – May 11, 1991

2 miscarriages

1-Maria de Jesus
2-Sara died as a baby
3-Maria Concepcion
4-Evangelina
5-Armando
6-Esperanza died as a baby
7-Alejandra
8-Maria
9-Lucia
10-José
11-Raul
12-Estela died as a baby
13-Rasa Maria
14-Leticia born 1957
15-Aida
16-Patricia
17-Ruben
18-Agueda

Yesterday 1

Chapter 1
Babies

Behind the curtain, midwife Dona Felix at her side, Mama screamed with each contraction, all of us children running about. We didn't care about the noise; we had heard such shouts of pain before, every nine months. After each birth, Papa would turn to Mama and ask, "Mama, es un niño?" But out of eighteen babies, Mama only had four boys.

I was one of the younger children, born in 1957, only four more babies were born after me, which makes thirteen babies born before me, although three died young.

Our house was small to hold all those babies, about six hundred square feet, but it wasn't unusual to have small houses and a lot of children in our village; it was the normal way.

We didn't have cribs for the babies back then, nothing like that. We had two sogas, pieces of rope, nailed from one corner of the room to the other, a blanket sewn from muslin for the baby to lie down in. Mama sewed it real good and put it close to the floor, not high, so she could rock it with her foot. She'd be breastfeeding one baby in her lap while swinging another with the push of her leg. When a new baby came along, my older sisters would take care of the older babies.

Mama never had disposable diapers, neither, not even cloth ones. She had farios, remnants of old clothes wrapped around the baby and tied with a ribbon. Like a belt. No pins. It was like an extra piece of material with a ribbon sewn at the end. That was the diaper. And washing the diapers, we were washing them all the time.

We'd stand over the pila—a cement square basin with a hole in the middle for the water to drain out of—and wash them there. But before the pila, we'd go to the river where we'd put all our clothes and farios on a rock, pour water over them, rub them hard with a bar of brown soap—the cheaper soap we had in Mexico—and then throw the wet clothes over the fence to dry. Once the clothes were dry, we'd take them home. If it rained, we'd hang them inside the house.

We went to the river every day, and if it wasn't me, it was someone else. Always, somebody had to go.

It seemed when one baby was born another was close behind. One baby at two years old would cry and ask for food, another would do the same; Mama would be breastfeeding another one.

There was always some kind of noise in our house, noise of babies, noise of chickens (which we sold at our house), people coming and going to buy the chickens. They'd want ten kilos of chickens and then we'd have to kill them. We could hear the neighbors, too. The walls were so thin we could hear their conversations, their arguments, behind our house and to the side of our house. Always the noise, everywhere.

Town, also. The clop, clop, clop of horses as men rode off to work, or the sound of a POP-the backfire of a car. Church bells ringing. Dogs barking. Doves cooing. Now and then we'd hear cows in nearby fields, or a pig squealing in the back of a pickup truck on its way to a carnicería to be butchered.

At night, there was the same noise, and in our house if it wasn't a newborn crying it was one of the other babies. They'd get sick or have a tummy ache because of Mama's milk because she had eaten something that wasn't good.

It was like our ears had never heard quiet before, in our house and our town, like we didn't know what silence was, like we never knew what it was like to hear nothing.

Like this is what it was to live in our town.

Chapter 2
Tomato Hair

Mama used to pull our hair back so tight you could see our faces stretched, or at least that's how it felt. She'd tie our hair with whatever ribbon was laying around, tug on it hard to get it straight. Papa never let us girls cut our hair, so our hair fell all the way down our backs. Mama was the only one in the family with short hair, short and curly.

If we were working in the fields with Papa, we needed to have our hair up. With Mama, she didn't want our hair hanging in the tortillas while we were making them, so we always braided our hair. The only time I remember *not* having our hair braided was when we went to the river and played.

Every day at the pila we washed our hair because we were dirty working in the fields. In winter, we washed it less. We used a jicara—a small bowl made from the calabash tree, a large round green fruit—to wash our bodies and hair. We'd dip the bowl that was like a hard gourd into the pila filled with cold water, and let the water run down our bodies. Because our hair was so long it took a long time to get the soap out of it, that brown bar of soap, the same one we used to wash our clothes.

We never had a lavadero naked. The girls wore a kind of slip that Mama made. I swear Mama just bought a piece of material, white cotton, and cut holes in it for arms. The boys wore undies. Mama and Papa never let the boys and girls bathe together. It was always separate.

The one thing we did get to decide for ourselves because Mama was always busy, was *when* to wash. I chose to bathe in the morning, four or six o'clock, sometimes later if I got busy doing things. Sometimes two or three of us would be standing together at the pila, us girls, and we'd start playing, throwing water at each other, things like that, like kids. I'd be the one to start that.

Sometimes we were late for school and in a hurry, so we'd brush each other's hair, like a little train, three or four sisters in a row, standing one behind the other. I often wonder if we might have all looked the same back then, standing in line with our brown eyes, dark skin, and long black braided hair.

To keep our hair from sticking out, to keep it close to the scalp, Mama would cut a tomato in half, cup it in her hand, and rub it over our heads. It was like a gel that made our hair shiny and smooth. Sometimes I could see the tomato seeds in my hair and I'd ask a friend, "Please, please, pull those things out!"

Mama and her ideas.

But looking back, I laugh at the thought. What if a little tomato patch could sprout and grow right out of the top of our heads.

Chapter 3
Period

Papa didn't like me doing boy things, like sports. No sports.
No jumping. If girls jumped, they might lose their virginity.
Girls riding bicycles could get pregnant. This is what we
thought.

Mama had a friend who was like a sister to her, Eliaser.
Mama and Eliaser even looked like sisters. They both had
high cheekbones as I have, and they both had a long narrow
face, were skinny, a little tall at 5'3" or so, with a short,
simple haircut, black and curly just above the shoulders.
They were different from each other, though. Eliaser told
things as they were, not lies like we were told by Mama.

Eliaser was strong and did what she wanted. If her
husband said, "Get me a tortilla," she said, "You want it,
you get it. There's your tortilla." She was the only woman I
knew who did things outside her house. She went to the
beach and the town pool with her children. She went to the
river where she taught me how to swim.

Eliaser is the one who helped me when I got my period.

"Eliaser, I think I'm pregnant!"

I was bleeding everywhere and thinking, *If I'm not
pregnant, I'm going to die.*

She started laughing.

"Leticia, you're not pregnant. You just started becoming a woman. That's normal. That will happen to you every month. It's your regla."

"But the blood is coming out. What do I do?"

"You need to wear only dresses. And use these."

Eliaser gave me rags and said I'd need to wash them.

"Wash them?"

Mama never talked to me about this kind of thing. Never. Menses was not a subject in *our* house. After I got my first period, I talked to my older sister.

"Does this happen to you?"

"Yes, of course."

"Then why didn't you tell me about it?"

"Because nobody is allowed to talk about it."

"I thought I was pregnant or going to die, and you didn't say nothing to me?"

I have two younger sisters and I told them about periods, because that first time I got up from my bed and there was blood everywhere and I was only twelve, I was more scared than I'd ever been.

When I came to the United States, I brought those rags with me and my older sister Eva looked at them with a scowl on her face.

"What are those?"

"Those are for my period."

"Oh Leticia, throw those away! This is not like our town in Mexico. Here in America it's different."

She brought me to the store to buy pads, and later when women used Tampax, I never used them. Why would I? I didn't want to put something like *that* inside me.

Chapter 4
Ten Minutes Before Ten

The only time we ever played was when Papa went to work on his evening shifts. He started at one in the afternoon and got home at ten at night. Mama was so tired all the time she would fall asleep in her chair, my cue to leave my sewing on the floor and run outside. My sisters rarely played outside because they listened to what Mama and Papa told them. Unlike me.

When I saw my friends doing fun things, I asked them, "Don't your parents get mad if you leave the house?"

"No," they'd say, which made me wonder, *Then, why can't I play? Why not me? I work hard. I get up at four in the morning. I go to bed late. I help with sewing and cleaning the house.*

I was always outside with Felix, one of my best friends. Her mother Eliaser was the woman across the street who taught me so much. We rolled marbles and pushed old tires down the streets, played games in a circle, took old metal lids and threw them like Frisbees. Whenever it rained, we'd make dams in the street with dirt and mud; then we'd have little rivers and puddles where we put sticks in them, like little floating boats.

My brothers, they left the house, too, and listened to a boy across the street, next door to Eliaser and her family, strum his guitar. They'd listen and sometimes they'd eat tacos or fruit or chicharrones. Music was their life. They'd do that until Papa got home.

At ten minutes before ten, my brother Raul and I would run back to our house, jump onto the big piles of corncobs that were our beds, pull the sheets over our bodies, and pretend that we had been asleep. Pretend that we had obeyed Papa. Pretend that we had never been outside. Pretend to be the good boys and girls he had hoped we would be.

Chapter 5
Pesos

One day Papa had been drinking but I didn't know he had been drinking. I asked him for some money to buy a dress like the girls at school. I kept asking for twenty pesos, only twenty pesos. My brother, Raul, heard my whining and told me to stop pestering Papa. Raul was always protecting me.

"You know what will happen, Leticia, leave him alone."

Papa was angry, even angry with Mama who had nothing to do with it.

"Maria, always girls! Why do you have so many girls? Some of those babies could have been strong handsome boys. But, girls! Girls don't work the same as boys. Girls aren't strong like a man. Girls want goddamn dresses!"

Papa finally did give me the money. He reached into his pocket, grabbed some coins, and threw them at my feet. Mama looked at me, looked at me hard, her eyes telling me to pick them up, pick them up or he'll do something.

"You know what, Papa? You know what? I want money to buy a dress. I want to look like the other girls. But I'm not going to do it like that. I'm not going to pick up that money. Why don't you just give it to me in my hands?"

I looked at Papa, right in his eyes.

"Don't talk back to me!" he said.

But I kept looking.

I guess Papa had had enough of my pestering and staring, so he did what he always did when we got angry. He raised his right hand and slapped me across my face. And then he left the room.

I bent down to the floor, noticed how the coins arranged themselves into a circle, like a shiny silver necklace. I thought how nice that would have been, to have a string of pesos around my neck, with a beautiful new dress.

Chapter 6
Punishment

My papa only punished a few of us, certainly Ruben; he was a troublemaker like me. He would pull at girls' dresses, put a mirror in his shoe so he could put it between a girl's legs, and look up there. He'd even try to sell us sisters: "Do you want my sister? How many pesos?" Then a boy would come up and say, "Your brother gave me five pesos, so now you're my girlfriend."

Ruben would steal food because we were hungry all the time. Whenever he did something like that, Papa would tie him to a chair with rope. I remember the marks on his body.

Once I went to a Quinceañera because I asked Papa in front of a friend if I could go. He said yes because she was standing there. As soon as I got home, he hit me with his belt. "Remember, Leticia, I told you I don't want any of your friends in my house, and I don't want you asking me permission with them right there. I have told you this before!"

At the table, Papa always ate first, then us, then Mama. He'd stand behind us with his belt in his hand, to be sure whatever food we had we ate. Especially at Easter. We weren't allowed to eat meat at Easter, only fish soup. But all that was in the soup were fish heads, and I didn't want to eat them. But then there was the belt.

The worst time with Papa, I was seven. My sisters Rosa and Aida—a year older and a year younger than me—and I went to my godfather's house to get some bread. I was hungry, and that's what my godfather did, he sold bread.

One day after church, since Papa wasn't with us—Papa never went to church but he made us go to catechism so we could do communion—I told Rosa and Aida I wanted to go to my padrino's house, only a five-minute walk from the church. I said this to my sisters because I'm not shy to ask for something. Rosa and Aida didn't want to go, but they went with me anyway.

Walking home, it was hard to hide the bread, so Papa knew right away what we had done. He learned we had asked my padrino for food, and for Papa, to ask for food was offensive; it hurt his pride. He didn't care which one of us had the idea, he just knew we had to be punished.

"On your knees," he said.

Once we were kneeling, he put a heavy brick in each of our arms and told us we needed to hold it for a long time. This was our punishment. For toda la noche.

Rosa and Aida didn't tell Papa it was my idea, but I knew what they were thinking; I could see it in their eyes.

I was the one who was always making the trouble.

Chapter 7
Raul

I admired the way he came to the United States and worked so hard. That was the time I saw Raul the most, when we were both in California. My family and I would go to St. Helena to see him and his family, and I'd bring Raul his favorite food. My husband, Ramiro, and I were living in Truckee then, so we'd drive from the snowy mountains of Tahoe to the green valley of Napa, a four-hour drive.

We ate together and drank together, Raul and I, we played cards. Sometimes we drank and talked until three in the morning. That was the best time. He was loving, and I was loving back. I'd come up from behind him and give him a hug. Only he and I did that.

Once after the mill had closed where Ramiro worked, Raul gave us a little money to get by on. That's how we were with each other.

I picture Raul in my mind during that time we were in Guadalajara. He was working there with his friend, Antonio, Eliaser's son. He was about fourteen and I was about twelve. I remember him as my handsome brother—tall, thin, short black hair, always dressed nicely, and always, always smiling or laughing.

We were in a park in Guadalajara, sitting on a park bench with Raul on one side of me and Antonio on the other.

They were starting to make plans to come to the United States.

"I feel bad, Leticia, but I need to go to the United States without you."

Raul didn't come to the United States until he was seventeen, but at fourteen he was already thinking about leaving Mexico.

"I want to do the same thing," I told him. "I want to go there, too."

"It's dangerous from what I hear. You need to be sure you've got money, you need to hide your money someplace they can't find it."

Raul was always protecting me and giving me advice.

Like the time I was going out with my first boyfriend, it was Raul who warned me.

"That guy's not good enough for you. You're better than that, Leticia. You're not a kid anymore."

"Why? Because I'm taller like you guys?"

I was tall and skinny as a kid, but even into my adulthood.

"No, because you're starting to have boyfriends. Think about the way you say you don't want to end up like Mama. Think about what you want to do with your life."

"You know why I got that boyfriend, Raul? I got him to give Papa a hard time. It's not because I love him. He's a drunk, he's lazy. Do you think I want to marry him? No way."

"Just never run away with him, OK?"

Most of the girls in my hometown were married by fourteen or fifteen. If you were sixteen or older, you were considered a solterona. "You will be a solterona the rest of your life," someone would say. "You will never marry."

"Raul! I'm not that miserable that I want to run away. My dreams are high. You can't even believe what my dreams are. *I never* want to be like Mama. I *never* want to have babies with that guy."

It was more like our conversations were about what was good for me and what was bad. Raul wanted to be sure before he left that I understood what mistakes I could make and what my life would look like with those mistakes. If I made a bad choice, I might not be able to go back and make a good one. What he was trying to tell me, I think, is that a *big* mistake could grab me so tightly it might never let me go.

Chapter 8
The Decision

I remember the day. I was twelve years old. It was 1969.

Papa and Mama were arguing, babies were crying because they're babies or because they're hungry. *I* was hungry. I stole tortillas because I was hungry, and then bread that time I got into trouble.

I was so hungry I just wanted to put something in my mouth but then there was nothing there. So I drank water. I drank, and drank, and drank, so I could get full. But ten or fifteen minutes later I'd just want to chew on something. My God! The noise in my stomach. Headaches, too, almost every day. Whenever I got my period...losing blood, working hard, hungry. Those three things together. It was like *How am I still here?*

We did have *some* food because we went to this plot of land where we planted corn and pepinos, squash, chiles, and beans. Not our own land, just a little area we went to, four or five miles out of town. Whoever got there first, it belonged to them; nobody said anything to you about going there.

Papa would say, "There are your rows, plant the corn there," and we'd start cleaning the ground, getting rid of the weeds, grasses, and bushes. We'd make a high row and a low row where the water could collect to soak the seeds.

After we cleaned the area, we got the azadón, a hoe-like tool, and scraped the ground to make the hole for the corn. "Put two seeds in each hole," Papa would say. And then we'd cover the hole by pushing the dirt into the hole with our shoes. But I'd put five seeds in a hole instead of two, to get rid of them faster because I wanted to finish planting, rapido, rapido. But Papa often caught me: "Leticia, what's happening here?"

On our way home, we carried corn on our backs and crossed the river with the big bundles, and it was hot and it was hard. Once at home, we had other things to do with the corn, like take off the kernels from the corncobs with our fingers (my fingers were always sore). Afterwards, Papa would put some kind of preservative on the kernels before dumping them into the barrels, so they would last a long time. Then he'd cover the barrels with heavy plastic, real tight so the corn wouldn't get wet. After we pulled out the corn, we'd cook it and take it to the Molino in town to be ground into masa to make the tortillas. We had tortillas all year long. Sometimes, we had elote and grilled the whole corn cob over a fire.

Those corncobs were our beds for a while, a stack of them before we got two beds where Aida, Rosa, Paty, and I slept in one, and Pepe, Ruben, and Raul slept in the other.

That day in 1969 when I was twelve years old, sitting outside our house and listening to all the arguing and the babies crying, I thought about being hungry, working in the fields, and the noise at home. I looked down at my dress with holes in it that Mama had covered with patches, the pattern so faded you couldn't see what it used to be. If a dress had flowers, you couldn't see the flowers. If a dress had a design, you couldn't see the design. Always I had hand-me-downs from my older sisters, which meant long dresses to just above our ankles, long dresses that I hated. Sometimes I shortened my dress on my way to school with a needle and thread, and then on my way home I'd pull the thread out and let my dress fall back to the ground again.

Our shoes were huarache sandals, leather, passed down from one to the other. Even the girls wore them though they were made only for hombres. Papa said the huaraches lasted the longest so that's what we wore. If something happened to those shoes, that was it, we were barefoot the rest of the year.

But even as we were poor we made money, other than what Papa brought home from the sugarcane factory. We sold fish and chicken we bought in Guzman, the fish kept in coolers with ice, the chickens alive and squawking.

In Guadalajara, we bought boxes and boxes of women's sandals, high heels and flats, to sell in our house, boxes piled one on top of the other, all the way to the ceiling. One of my jobs was to collect the money for the shoes, week by week. For a pair of shoes that cost 45 pesos I'd collect 5 pesos, then 5 more, 10, 15, until the shoes were all paid for.

All these things I was thinking about on the curb in front of our house that day. Poverty. But I didn't know the name then.

I started to notice it didn't matter where I went in town, everything was the same. The families were the same, the children were the same. I saw thirteen and fourteen-year-old girls run away with their boyfriends because that was normal. I saw families with so many children running around because that was normal. I saw women not being

41

able to get out of their houses until their husbands went with them. I saw men with other women, not their wives. I mean, why? What was for me?

Tell me, Guadalupe! Why can't Mama stop having babies? Why are Mama and Papa always arguing?

I was angry at Mama, and I was angry at Papa, especially Papa who always argued with Mama. Maybe that's why I always disobeyed him.

This is when everything began in me. I don't know why I was thinking these things at such an early age, but I remember that day, and I knew, *something has to change.*

I made a decision, even though I had no answer. Not at twelve years old. But I knew this wouldn't be *my* life, not with feeling like nothing…not with all that emptiness inside.

Chapter 9
Three Days and Three Nights

I had been waiting for the question for a very long time, and at fourteen I was even more ready to answer it.

"Leticia, can you come to California to help me with my children?"

That's what my sister Eva asked me when she was visiting our hometown in Mexico one time.

"Yes!" I immediately answered, "Eva, I have been waiting for somebody to come get me. Yes! Yes!"

I ran to Papa to tell him what Eva had said.

"I want to go, Papa. I want to go to the United States. I want to help take care of Eva's children."

"OK, Leticia. Goodbye then. I'm free of you."

That's what he said, and that I was a difficult child because of the way I was with him. That I never respected him. That I talked back to him. And he was right. I *didn't* respect him. I *did* talk back to him because he punished me for no reason.

"I'm happy you're not going to give me trouble anymore," Papa said.

That was my dream, to get out of town. The best opportunity came, so that's why I said yes, without hesitation.

Mama didn't have a voice in the situation. She couldn't say yes or no, only, "Leticia, if that's what you want, and

43

you feel you can handle it, that's fine. I hope you can do a good job there."

The day before I left I had a party with my girlfriends— Felix, Chayo, Alicia, Martha, Alejandra, Elpidia, Maricela, Licho, and Bertha. We met at the village pool and everybody brought food and punch with tequila, "ponche" we call it, alcohol with fruit. It wasn't unusual to drink tequila at such a young age. We all started drinking when we were ten, ponche, but beer and brandy also. Felix gave me a big hug and looked into my eyes, "That's the best for you, Leticia. All of us want to do that someday."

We were always there to support each other.

One friend was worried though, about immigration and money: "Remember, Leticia, you will be stuck in the house because you don't have papers. And what if your sister doesn't give you any money?"

I was worried, too, but only that I wouldn't have this opportunity again.

"I have to go."

The day before we left Eva told me to pack three changes of clothes and one pair of shoes, which are all the shoes I had anyway. Also, to bring a plastic bag in case we needed to cross a river.

Sometimes you don't know how you're going to cross the border.

I was scared about leaving but happy at the same time. I changed from laughing to crying and then laughing again. The night before I left I didn't sleep. The next morning at five o'clock Eva came to pick me up.

"Papa and Mama, goodbye," I shouted to no one.

Papa didn't say anything; he never got out of bed. I went to Mama and hugged her, and she made a sign of the cross in the air in front of her body. She wanted to cry but she didn't. I wanted to cry, too, but I held it in. I didn't want to cry in front of Mama.

My brothers and sisters didn't say anything either. Raul would have said something, had he been there, but he was already living in the United States. He was the only one who would have said goodbye and wished me luck.

As soon as I got in the car I cried, at the same time I watched Mama walk back to the outdoor hallway that led to our house. In that moment, I thought about where she lived but mostly *how* she lived, working all the time, and Papa, Papa hitting her. *Would Mama be okay?*

Eva and her husband José, who we called Pepé, and their five children and I, packed into their blue Dodge station wagon with our clothes, blankets, and a cooler with food.

We drove out of Vista Hermosa, passed the sugarcane fields, passed the roadside stands of fruit and drinks, passed the donkeys and horses in the road, passed people walking to work.

As we were driving, I didn't want to have that feeling of being sorry for what I had done, so I never looked behind the car out the back window; I only looked out front.

I was on my way to America, I kept telling myself. *You can do it. You can do it. You can do it.*

I had never been farther away than an hour from my hometown, so I figured the United States was about that same distance, thirty minutes or so, an hour at the most, not three days and three nights. After one day of driving with my sister, brother-in-law, and their five children, I panicked. I was fourteen years old, a young girl.

That first day was the hardest because of the children, three, four, five, six, and eight—the crying, the smell of their poo, all of us cramped together in the car. It was hard because I'm not a person to sit down for so long. I am a person moving around and helping Mama. To sit for hours and hours was difficult.

The first night, how hard it was. We were far away from Vista Hermosa, farther than I thought we could ever be. *Would I ever go back home again?* I didn't know what to expect as we got closer and closer to the border. *Would immigration officers stop us and put me in jail? Would I never see my family in Mexico again? What would the United States be like?*

Eva tried to calm me down.

"Leticia, if you want to go back, we can take you back."

"No, Eva, I made my decision. I just need to know how far it is. It's already been twenty-four hours and you keep saying there's more driving."

I felt lonely, empty, even as I was with my sister.

Along the way we never stopped at a hotel because Eva and Pepé couldn't afford one, so we slept in the car instead. She brought an ice chest with ham and bread and everything we'd need. But I barely ate. I just kept thinking, *How am I going to pass the border? What's going to happen to me*?

Then there it came, the country I had longed to live in for so long. The United States. Sitting right next to Tijuana.

Tijuana had people everywhere. People in the street with trinkets to sell, hanging on every part of their body— wool blankets draped over their shoulders, beaded bracelets and necklaces lined up from their wrists to their elbows, straw hats piled on top of one another, a whole stack sitting on top of a man's or a woman's head. Kids, too, were walking in the streets, some kids sitting in wheelchairs, some without shoes. I saw men and women with missing limbs, selling food in cups, selling pictures, selling Tijuana souvenirs.

I looked at the freeways with so many cars, flowers in the middle of the freeways, trees in the middle. All the people. I kept asking myself, *Why am I here?*

But the same answer always came to me: I am here *not* to be like Mama. I kept repeating that over and over to myself. I don't want to get married, have so many children, have a husband who's going to be a drunk all day like Papa. That is not who I want to be, home all the time, feeding my husband, feeding my children. I was tired of seeing people in my town, walking without shoes, with sadness on their faces.

It was time to cross the border, and I was worried about getting my sister and brother-in-law in trouble. At the same time, there we were. What was I going to do? Turn around? After three days and three nights? I knew I needed to cross, but I had no idea what problems were on the other side.

Chapter 10
Crossings

The first time I crossed the border, Eva, Pepé, and their five children drove into California and left me behind in Tijuana. No coat. No gloves. No hat. Freezing. It was scary because men were looking at me.

I was with Eliaser's sister in Tijuana while Eva and her family were on the other side. Eva was going to give her visa to our brother Armando who was waiting at the border in the U.S.; he was legal there. He would then cross back into Mexico and pass me Eva's visa.

While I waited with Eliaser's sister, she put makeup on me and gave me a wig so I'd appear older, so that I'd look like Eva.

Armando found me right away in Tijuana and gave me Eva's visa and we quickly crossed the border into San Diego.

At the San Diego airport, getting ready to fly to Sacramento to meet Eva (I couldn't get in the car with them because there was a second immigration stop in San Clemente) I went into the bathroom. Just after I came out, there was immigration.

I don't know how they knew I wasn't legal, but I learned later that immigration is everywhere and they just know. They dress in regular clothes so you don't suspect who they are.

The immigration man grabbed my visa: "What's your husband's name?" referring to Pepé. I told him. "And his age?" That's how immigration got me. I didn't know Pepe's age. I had to admit I was lying, but I didn't admit the visa was Eva's. "I stole the visa. I don't know who it belongs to." Eva and I had planned that just in case so Eva wouldn't get in trouble.

After that, immigration took me to jail in San Diego. For one night. Only one night. I wasn't scared like I thought I would be.

Once Eva was in the United States, she reported she had lost her visa.

The next morning, immigration sent me back to Tijuana. Eliaser's sister picked me up, and I stayed with her and her family for a month because I needed to wait for immigration to forget about me, even as they had taken my picture and fingerprints.

The second time I crossed the border, I went with Jorge, a family friend who lived in Los Angeles. I used one of his children's visa's. While we crossed, I pretended to be asleep in the back seat, scared they'd ask questions since I didn't know English. Jorge told the border patrol I had a temperature and that I needed to get to the United States, soon. Luckily, they let us go.

When you're in America you have to check-in at immigration. At San Clemente, there was no one there to inspect us. "We need to cross *now*, Leticia," Jorge said. "Nobody's here."

So that was a success. I was now in the United States!

For two years, I lived with Eva and Pepé and their children in Sacramento, and everything was good. But then more trouble. A neighborhood friend had reported me to immigration. Another Mexican! A Mexican friend of the same age as me, sixteen. I don't know if she was jealous or resented that I worked in the fields and made more money than her. I don't know the reason, but she was the one who turned me in.

It happened at seven o'clock in the morning just as I was getting Eva's children ready for school. She and Pepé had left for work. After I opened the front door, there they were.

"We're immigration. We need to see your papers."

I called a neighbor to call my sister and asked the neighbor if she would come over and watch the children.

The immigration man made me go to jail in Sacramento where I spent two nights. This time I was scared, but also angry. *Who would do this to a friend?*

While I was in jail, immigration was waiting to have enough illegal people to fill up a bus to go back to Tijuana. So, back to Tijuana I went.

"Stay close to the border," Eva said. "We're going to pick you up, Leticia. We want to try again. We're going to do it this time."

The third time I crossed the border I had "coyotes" help me in the hills near Tijuana. We crossed a river, I think it was this third time, but it wasn't a big river, only up to our knees. It wasn't bad like I thought it would be.

It was like a day and a half before I got to somebody's house where they hid me and others. They hid us and moved us from one house to another. It was maybe five houses before I got to my sister. The coyotes got in touch with her and told her where to meet me. "Go to this place and you will find your sister."

After this, Eva decided it wasn't safe for me in Sacramento.

My next place was San Jose where I lived for a year with a friend of Eva's, Irene, and her two children. I took care of those two children, just as I had taken care of Eva's five. At night, I went to school to learn English.

After that year, I moved back in with Eva and her family in a new house. But Eva and Pepé worried I'd have more problems with immigration, plus I was having nightmares from all those years. They knew there was only one option left to keep me in the United States, one more thing to try.

I had to get married, and they knew a man who would do it, who would agree to be my husband.

Chapter 11
A False Marriage

He was a veteran, a nice man. He was in a war, maybe World War II; I don't know. He was forty to forty-five years older than me, a Mexican, a United States citizen.

Pepé had a contract with Julian for him to marry me. We paid him three to five thousand dollars, which was a lot of money back then. I was seventeen; Julian would have been about sixty. He signed the contract, and Eva and Pepé signed the contract, too, because I was underage. We got married in Reno, I don't remember where; there were so many places to do that.

Julian was a big man, heavy, maybe 250 pounds, about average height, always dressed neatly in his shirt tucked into his pants. Short straight dark hair, combed. I was lucky Julian never tried to do anything with me, nothing at all, not even a kiss. When we'd meet, we'd shake hands.

Before we got married, we met about four or five times to ask each other questions that immigration might ask us— What side of the bed does each of you sleep on? What clothes does Julian normally wear? What is his favorite color? What are his hobbies? What is his favorite food? What are your pet names for each other, like honey, or something like that. What are the names of your brothers and sisters? We had to be prepared.

When it came time to face immigration after all the studying of one another, they never asked us anything, and I got my green card right away. I've always wondered if it was because Julian went to war, because he was a veteran.

We waited six months before we got a divorce because you don't do it right away. Then I needed to have my green card for ten years to go in and out of the United States, back and forth to Mexico, to be able to stay in the United States. This was the time I visited Salvador, my boyfriend back in Mexico, and the time I studied for my GRE and passed the test, which I took in Mexico. Later, I studied for my citizenship and passed that too.

My God! Those years!

What would Mama and Papa think of me now? I remember thinking. I had changed from a young girl to a young woman.

I had spent nights in jail.

I had crossed a small river.

I had moved from one house to another before my sister could come get me.

I had married a man I didn't love just to get to a place I knew I needed to be.

I had worked several jobs, taken care of children, learned how to speak English.

I, the troublemaker, had settled in a new country. By my own will and determination.

I was a survivor. Didn't they see that?

What was it Papa used to say?

"Why so many girls, Maria? Why not boys? Boys are strong like a man."

Chapter 12
United States

So many things were different in the United States.

I remember the first time I walked into a clothing store, my thoughts ran from *Oh, my God! Women can wear jeans and shorts?* To *Women can wear high heels?* While I observed people driving, I thought, *Women in beautiful cars, driving? Women can drive cars?*

The first McDonald's I went to was in San Diego. People were coming and going, everybody, women and children. In my hometown, we never went out to eat, never. We might have had a taco on the street or bought some bread, but we never went to a restaurant. We didn't even know what a restaurant was. After McDonald's, I knew; *I want to eat this kind of food all the time*.

Close to Sacramento I saw many towns, small towns. But every time I saw a police car I was sure, *Oh my God, that's immigration. They're going to get me. They're going to send me back to Mexico*. Still, even at fourteen, even being scared, I knew, *This United States. This is for me*.

I cooked and cleaned and did everything I could do to help Eva and Pepé's children. I was their nanny and they called me "Mama." I learned English by sitting in the back of one of the child's kindergarten classes. I did that four to five days a week when time allowed. But every time I walked to school with the children and saw a policeman, I was scared, until a neighbor said, "Leticia, policemen don't pick you up. Immigration is one thing and policemen are another." I felt comfortable after that.

I wanted to help my family in Mexico, and the best way was to think about myself first. What could I do in the United States to help them? That's what kept me going.

At sixteen, I had two jobs, the first was working in the tomato fields from midnight to 6:00 a.m. Because it was dark, the tomato fields were bright with lights so we could see the tomatoes we picked up and down the rows. My second job was working at a laundry, a big company where they sent clothes to a hospital; I ironed blouses and shirts. I was doing well at the laundry, so they sent me to a different department where I organized orders, like putting a hundred towels into one basket. I was working ten hours a day and making twice more than other people. I could help my family just like I wanted to.

I started wearing jeans and shaving my legs because I hadn't done that in Mexico; I even bought a bra. I imagined what Papa would think seeing me in different clothes, how he'd be mad. But then I'd remember, *He's not looking at you, so it doesn't matter*. Still, I thought of my family all the time, hoping they had something to eat; I knew how hard it was.

I imagined, also, what my sisters would think of me, living in a different country. I believe they didn't think there was another life out there. They didn't look farther than their own houses. From what I saw during that time I lived in our little town in Mexico, my sisters didn't want anything different.

They didn't want to be somebody else.

Yesterday 2

Chapter 13
Boyfriends

Even though I had been living in California, I traveled back and forth to Vista Hermosa after I became legal. That's how I started dating Salvador.

I liked Salvador, a lot. He wasn't a drunk like most boys I knew in Mexico, but he was a real spoiled guy. He caught the attention of a lot of girls because he was so handsome. He had a muscular body like a soccer player, six feet tall, black curly hair, with the deepest green eyes, bright as a sugarcane leaf after the rain. Salvador was four years older than me.

I visited Salvador every time I went to Mexico. He even came to California once to see me. We wrote letters and talked on the phone. I was in love with the guy, and we were going to get married. One day Salvador said to me on the phone, "I don't want to get married in a church, Leticia, let's just go to Reno." I knew my papa wouldn't like that idea, but I said, OK, we'll go to Reno.

I told my papa we were going to get married, but the instant I told him I knew something was wrong.

"First, Leticia, we're going to sit down, and then after I tell you what I know about your boyfriend you can decide what you want to do."

This is how Papa did things. Straightforward. I didn't understand until much later that being direct was his way of teaching us the hard things in life.

"Your boyfriend, or your husband if you decide to marry him, is living with that lady in Guadalajara."

"I know that, Papa."

I knew Salvador was living with a woman from our hometown. That woman lived in Vista Hermosa when I was a kid, and I sold her some of our chickens every Sunday, brought them to her house. Her son was Salvador's best friend, like brothers. They were always together, playing sports, going to the same school; they even looked alike. Her son died at nineteen years old and after that she moved to Guadalajara. Salvador decided to continue his education there and went to college to study architecture and moved into her house. She had three daughters and a husband who worked in the United States.

"Papa, I know he's living with that lady. Why are you telling me this?"

Papa said he had Salvador's address, and if I wanted to go and check for myself, he'd take me there.

"I don't want you to make a mistake in your life because Salvador doesn't have the guts to tell you."

"Tell me what? I already know."

"No, you don't know."

"Yes, I do."

"No, you don't."

"Don't know what?"

"Let me tell you then. He got a little girl with that person. Leticia, that little girl is already three."

60

How can I express how I felt when he told me that. Was it true?

Even though Papa offered to drive me to Guadalajara, he didn't. I went with one of my older sisters, Rosa, who assured me what Papa said was the truth.

After we arrived in Guadalajara, we went to the house where the lady and Salvador lived. Right in front of that lady, he said he was never serious about me. I couldn't believe he said that; we were going to get married.

I only had three boyfriends in my life. Of course, the first one really wasn't a boyfriend; I was only twelve and he was fourteen. I was more like testing to see how it was. He was a drunk. We all drank as young children, starting at ten, tequila of course. Most girls would say, "What can I do with this guy?" But I wanted to do things differently. If a boy came to my house and I could smell he had been drinking, I'd tell him to leave. I wasn't going to lose my tongue with him.

Then there was Salvador, who took me a long time to get over. And then Ramiro.

When I met Ramiro, I didn't trust him at first because of Salvador, but Ramiro knew how much Salvador had hurt me, so he told me what I needed to hear: "You know, Leticia, not everybody's the same. I won't leave you."

I saw that little girl in Guadalajara, the day I visited Salvador. I saw her in the living room of that lady's house. She was sitting on the floor playing with a doll and talking to it while brushing its hair. I stood there and stared at her because I didn't know what else to do. She was a pretty little girl, black curly hair falling down her back. But the thing

61

that kept me looking at her were her eyes. She had the most beautiful green eyes. Just like his.

Chapter 14
Marriage

In 1978, I was visiting Vista Hermosa where we both grew up, but I never met Ramiro in my village before because he's fifteen years older than me. I was only two. I met him much later at a friend's wedding in our hometown.

In our early years together, Ramiro had long hair, not too long since it was curly. He wore it in a small afro and he had a bushy mustache; it was the seventies. I told him I didn't like the mustache, but he kept it anyway. Soon after we met at the wedding in December, he asked me if I'd be his girlfriend, on February 14th, Valentine's Day. I said yes, and later that year, in 1979, we got married.

For a living, Ramiro's parents killed cows and pigs and sold the meat. I told my sisters—I was twenty-two years old at the time—"I'm going to marry the meat man." They were excited because we were always hungry and they thought when Ramiro visited Vista Hermosa he would bring them pieces of cows and pigs. One of my sisters married a guy who sold taquitos; they were excited about that too.

Papa always told us we could never run away with a boyfriend, *never*. That we needed to ask permission to get married, that the boy would have to come to him. My sister Alejandra ran away with her boyfriend, to Guzman, only an hour away from our town. I don't know the age she did that, but she wasn't allowed to go back home. After five years, she finally returned, but when she did my papa tried to kill her, I mean kill her. He went around Alejandra's neck and tried to choke her with his hands. My oldest sister Concha got in the way and stopped him. That's the worst thing I remember Papa doing.

Ramiro went to Papa to ask if he could marry me, and Papa said yes, but he also said, "You need to be careful with Leticia. She can be trouble. All my life I cannot control her. You need to be tough with her because she will do whatever she wants. You need to show her how it is with a man and woman." He told Ramiro I was a disappointment. A disappointment!

Later he had a talk with me too. "When Ramiro doesn't show up one night, the next morning you will receive him as if nothing happened." He was talking about my husband sleeping with other women. I said yes, Papa, I would receive him, but I was telling a lie. I would never accept a man who had been with another woman.

After Papa and I talked, I sat down with Ramiro. "We live in the United States, and we will live for ourselves. It's not like your word will be the last, Ramiro, not like my papa or your papa."

I asked Papa if he would bring me to the church on my wedding day, but he found out Ramiro had been married before, so he said no, he would not come.

The day of my wedding I waited outside the church in my wedding dress, very traditional, long sleeves, high at the neck, pink and white—those were the colors of the flowers in my hair and my bouquet. Mama's dress was pink, too, dusty rose, nothing fancy, long to the ground, the same as

Ramiro's mother. My aunts and uncles, nephews, nieces, cousins, everyone was there. Except Papa.

I looked up at the sky that afternoon, at the top of the third-story bell tower and above that, the blue and white dome that pronounced the big red-brick church, the highest building in town. I thought of Guadalupe, the Virgin Mary, and I had a little talk with her, in private. "Guadalupé," I said, "I will be a married woman soon. I will be Ramiro's wife and living in the United States. We will work hard and be good and have children."

I was praying to the Virgin Mother, but my mind was thinking of other things, too, of my life *before* Ramiro. Like when I was a little girl, out on the street rolling tires with a stick. Swimming in the river. The bright pink bougainvillea trees, shelter from the heat. How, at night we walked around the square, always in the same direction like a clock, the girls arm in arm while the boys watched our nightly strolls. I was thinking of Concha, Eva, Raul, Maria, Lucia, José, Esperanza, Armando, all my brothers and sisters. Our neighbors like Lupé, the woman across the street who made the tortillas with her daughter, and Eliaser, who was like Mama's sister. I was thinking of Mama cooking rice, the cones of piloncillo set to the side. I was thinking of the sugarcane fields burning and that sweet burnt smell that lingered all day. The boyfriend who was no good. Mama having babies. Catechism. Being hungry. All those things.

But then I had to stop remembering because I heard organ music, and I knew it was time for me to go. It was time to marry my Ramiro.

I took my eyes away from the top of the church and was getting ready to walk up the steps, but then I saw a man walking up the street toward me, seeming familiar, but I didn't know who it was. Until he got closer.

"Papa!"

He didn't say nothing, nothing at all, but he smiled, and that was good enough. Papa, in a new suit, took hold of my arm, and we walked into the church together.

Chapter 15
Gaby

We called her Chuy, my oldest sister, the first one in the family, but her real name was Maria de Jesus. In Mexico, everybody was Maria—because of the Virgin Mother—Maria this, Maria that. Chuy wanted to be a nun, but Papa said no, women can't do that, which I didn't understand because we were Catholic and we believed in religion. Instead of being a nun, Chuy got married and then she got pregnant, and then another year later she got pregnant again.

On Christmas Eve 1965, Chuy ended up in the hospital; this was during her second pregnancy; she was about four and a half months along. Because it was a holiday, it was quiet, not many people around.

The way I heard it, a staff member at the hospital found her in the hallway, bleeding uncontrollably. Chuy was having a miscarriage.

Later that day, it's hard to believe, but Chuy died.

Chuy's daughter Gaby was three years old when her mama and the baby died, so I was hired to help to take care of Gaby, alongside her papa, abuela, and tia, even as I was only eight.

I always picture Gaby walking with her face down. No Mama. Living with her old abuela. Always quiet. I think of her with her hair in a ponytail or sometimes loose to her shoulders. A pretty girl, but sad.

The thing I remember most were the walks in the hills; she loved to explore. She was a smart kid too, all the way through school. Just as soon as she was old enough, her papa sent her to college in Guadalajara where she majored in Industrial Engineering. He wanted her to continue her education, unlike my papa who never sent any of us to college. During that time Gaby was in college, and I was older, I went to visit her in Guadalajara because Salvador was there also.

But life takes the strangest turns.

One day while Gaby was washing clothes at her college—she was twenty—she became unconscious and fell on the cement floor. I think she was exhausted and weak from all her studying and working so hard. She hit her head, that's all she did. But two hours later, I couldn't believe something like this could happen to someone so young. Gaby died too, just like her mama and baby.

Gaby's funeral was the first funeral I went to, a big one, maybe three hundred people. There were one hundred alone from Guadalajara, all her friends from college, and then all the people from our town. I was there with my newborn son, only two months old.

After the service in Vista Hermosa, they drove her body to Zapotiltic, fifteen minutes from Vista Hermosa, where people visited and brought flowers. I'd never seen so many flowers in my life.

After Gaby's funeral, I sat down with Mama, friends, and my siblings, and we talked about why we never got close to Gaby. My sister Rosa was close to her, a little, because she moved to Guadalajara. She would take her to a movie or out to dinner. Other than Rosa, the rest of my family didn't do much for her. I don't know why.

Gaby was the first girl I saw who did what she wanted. She went to college. She studied engineering. No one told her she couldn't be who she wanted to be. No one told her "No."

Chapter 16
They Call Me Tecia

It might seem strange to some people, those who have never been hungry or without love, the reason I started a daycare and then a preschool. For me, as a child, I was always hungry and lived in a house that didn't show affection. That's the reason I work with children. I figured I could feed them and I could love them. They call me Tecia, all the children, and I love them like they're my own.

After I got married, I had two children and then I got pregnant with my third. I stayed home for a while, but then I saw how many parents, both parents, in our town, worked. So, I started taking in children at my daycare business, and two years later I accepted more.

I have a one hundred percent Spanish immersion program at my business. I know how, in other countries, like France, Japan, even Mexico, they offer four or more languages. Here in the United States, I don't understand why children only speak English. In having a second language, they could have more opportunities for jobs. We can also teach children not to be racist, to accept color.

I've been taking care of children all my life, ever since I helped with Eva's five children in Sacramento and Irene's two children in San Jose. Being a caregiver is what I do. Through the years, many of the families at my daycare and preschool have become a part of my family, something special I didn't foresee.

God gave me the gift to be with children, to teach them, to love them, to give them a good foundation, so when they leave me they'll feel strong, not like when I moved to the United States at fourteen. My childhood was lonely, and I didn't want these children to experience that.

Raising my own children, I wanted to give them opportunities to be educated and to play sports. If they wanted to go to college, we'd support them to do that. We tried to give them what they needed as they were growing up, but not too much. At fourteen and sixteen, my children worked part-time.

Mama didn't think that way of course. She didn't think her children needed anybody. That time Papa was helping Lucia, financially, because she was sick, Mama said, "You don't need to help her. I don't understand why you buy her groceries. She needs to work. When I was young, nobody gave *me* anything." How cold she was. No affection. No love. But I never put together that Mama was that way because she was working all the time.

For me, an important part of raising my children was simple things like teaching them to set the table, pick up the dishes, make their own room, take out the garbage. This way they learn how to help. And it's the best way to communicate, to talk to each other. In the kitchen, in the dining room.

I talked to my three children about those things Mama and Papa never talked about—sex, menses, consequences if my daughter got pregnant or if my sons got a girl pregnant. I talked to my daughter about being equal to boys, told her she could do what they do: play sports, volunteer, go to college, have a career. This was never talked about in *my* home.

But the thing I gave my children that was missing the most for me, was love. Hugging. Kissing. Being on the floor, playing. Whenever I changed a diaper, I talked and sang to my children, something Mama never did. She didn't touch our faces, she didn't talk. I think that's where it starts, such a simple thing, changing a diaper. To me, that was a special time to touch my baby. And look straight into my baby's eyes. That was the most important thing of all. Looking at them and having them look back at you.

Chapter 17
José Parra in Jail

Two years before Papa passed away, my sister Concha told me a story about how Papa ended up in jail, how her son-in-law got involved in that time.

Concha has a daughter that is married, and Papa sold his old truck to that guy. When he sold the truck, Papa never changed the name of the owner because he was family, which is how Papa got into trouble. He didn't know that Concha's son-in-law had had problems with the law.

One day, a judicial found drugs inside the truck and arrested Papa. The judiciales is a division of law enforcement in charge of drugs. They carry big guns and wear heavy boots and bulletproof vests. One of them tied Papa's hands behind his back and made him walk through town so everybody could see him. Before they took him to jail, they grabbed Mama and pushed her to the floor.

While Papa was in jail, they kept asking him if the drugs were his, but the police in Mexico, you know, they're different from the ones in America. You cannot answer them, you cannot talk to them, you just need to be quiet. Whatever they are doing to you, you don't answer.

In jail, the judicial got a woman from another cell and brought her to Papa.

"If you don't tell the truth, José, we will cut her breast."

My papa didn't know what to do.

"But I don't have anything to do with that. That's not my truck. I sold it to my daughter's son-in-law."

"But it's in your name," the judicial said.

So that's the mistake my papa made; he never changed the name.

One day they lead that woman again to my papa and asked him again to tell them about the drugs, but he kept saying they weren't his, he did nothing wrong. They didn't believe him so they took that woman and they did it, right in front of him. With a knife. They cut her breast.

Three days later some people from our town who knew Papa got him out of jail. They knew he was innocent. But he was suffering. Not having respect was the most painful thing.

After that time, my papa got sick and could not sleep. He could not sleep, he could not eat. He started having cirrhosis, because, you know, the stress. Two years after that happened, while I was sitting next to him when he was passing away, he was crying, crying hard.

He was remembering that time in jail.

He was remembering that woman.

Chapter 18
Papa's Last Words

You'd think my story would be mostly about Mama, the woman who had had eighteen children and tried her best to keep up the house with all the noise in it. But my story is a lot about Papa too because he was the one in control. Because of that, Mama never said much; she wasn't allowed to. She wasn't allowed to go outside, only if she was with Papa buying shoes or fish or things like that. She was always behind the doors.

It was only until the last month of his life that Papa changed. I was with him during that time, and he told me a lot of things that helped me understand him.

Maybe Papa was Papa because of his beginning, born from a mother who didn't know who her son's father was. All his mama said was she was "abused" by several men and got pregnant. I think this was always hard on him, Papa not having a daddy. During his last days before he died, he begged Mama to tell him about his father, but she didn't want to say what she knew.

Papa was a handsome man—tall, dark hair, bushy black mustache, strong. How I describe Papa, is…very specific. He had to have Mama iron his clothes every day, his khaki pants pressed with a perfect crease running down the middle, the collars on his white, blue, or brown shirts pressed just right. His red bandana handkerchief that he stuffed into his back pocket all the time, it had to be ironed too. He shaved every morning with a bar of soap and a knife to his chin and brushed his teeth every night with baking soda so they'd stay white. Remembering Papa, I see him walking upright.

He had to eat before his children and certainly before Mama. "I'm done with my Caguama," he'd say to Mama, as he moved the big 40 oz. bottle of beer to the side, the signal to bring his meal.

He was particular about Mama, only Mama could feed him.

He was particular about everything.

Once, when I was visiting from the United States, I wanted to cook for Papa because I had learned how to cook. But when I gave him his salad, he yelled, "I don't want that salad. I want your mama to cook. I don't want your food. And this is not the time I eat. I'm drinking my beer right now!"

"Papa, I'm trying to show you what I learned and how I changed these past three years."

Only Mama knew the right time to put the dish in front of Papa, nobody else.

Even as Mama worked hard all her life, she never got any thanks from Papa for anything she did, "No, not at all. Totally quiet," she told me after I asked if Papa ever praised her for anything.

Although he was a hard man, Mama said she never would have left Papa, even as he brought other women…into our house! She said that when you get married they tell you that you have to be faithful until death. Even with sickness you have to stay together. Papa didn't think about leaving either. But she said she thinks differently now, that if a man is having relationships with other women they should not stay together.

I learned from my sisters that before I was born Papa ran away with another woman while still married to Mama. He disappeared for a year! He took his money and left Mama in the street with no house, no nothing. She had maybe six children by then.

Papa did come back after all that time, Mama living in a house with a poor family who invited her to stay, one room with two families.

During that period Papa was away, one of my brothers, Armando, was sick and needed surgery. To help with the medical bills, but also to help feed the family, Mama and my siblings worked extra jobs. Mama sold chicken and fish. That was the hardest time, my sisters told me.

Papa was a proud man. Even while he was dying he didn't admit to dying. If someone from work came by to visit and asked how he was, he'd say, "A little better now." He was certain he'd improve and return to work. He was convinced he'd never die.

During that last month when I was with Papa, he got thin and weak, so I tried to help with small jobs around the house, like painting. I knew how he had to have everything perfect, and since he taught me how to paint as a child, that was the one thing I could do for him. "OK, honey, go get some paint," he said.

Before he died, he talked about that time he was put in jail by the police and being so ashamed he was arrested, with handcuffs around his wrists, how everyone was staring at him. He was also thinking about that woman in jail with him, the woman who suffered so much. Mama said he didn't sleep after that and got sick a year later.

Ruben and I were the only ones who turned our time around with Papa, made our relationships better. It was important for us to see another Papa, even if it was at the end of his life. I asked Papa why he did the things he did.

"I did some things wrong, Leticia. I didn't have the knowledge on how to raise children. The way I treated you, the way I hit you, the way I was happy you left the house to go to the United States with your sister—it was the only way I knew. I feel angry for what I did. I feel embarrassed. It was the way I was raised and the way I was drinking, did things to your mama. I did some mistakes in my life. Will you forgive me?"

Papa was crying.

"You know, Papa. I'm not mad at you. I don't have anything against you. I have my own children now and I'm learning how to raise them. Nobody's perfect, I can tell you that. Think positively, Papa. I do love you."

Papa smiled. He couldn't say anything else.

That last month of Papa's life turned everything around for Papa and me. I finally got to talk to him and ask him questions, to tell him I loved him.

I got to know a different Papa.

Chapter 19
Money

Mama's house had only one bedroom, not much there. It was small for all those children and Papa and Mama. When Mama got older, I remember thinking *Who will support my old mama when she gets sick?* I sent Mama money all the time, but I never saw anything new in her house or things she could use to improve her life. "Mama, what do you do with the money I send you?"

"Medication," she said, "I need medication."

In Mexico, when a husband passes away he leaves all his money to his wife. Mama didn't know Papa had money, but after he died in 1991 at the age of seventy-four he left her $100,000 pesos; that's about $5,000 American dollars. Mama was only seventy then.

Mama started changing after she received that money.

Mama started buying jewelry because she never had jewelry. She bought dresses because she never had store-bought dresses, only dresses sewn from material my papa bought for her and all us kids. Papa always wanted Mama dressed in dark colors, I don't know why, so after he died she wore light, bright colors like red, pink, and purple. She bought shoes. She bought makeup. She had pedicures and manicures. Every time somebody from the United States went back to Mexico she wanted something nice to wear and some jewelry to go with it.

She traveled, too, on a bus...to Michoacán, Cancun, Puerto Vallarta, Acapulco. Lucia or Concha or Maria would go with her. She was a little older than seventy when she started traveling. She traveled to the United States once when Papa was still alive, to help me with my youngest son Ramiro. After Papa died, she came to help Raul who was sick, and then she came to his funeral. After that, she came to my house every year. Her most favorite memory was the seventieth celebration I gave her, the first birthday party she had ever had.

That first year after Papa died Mama didn't spend the money; she was afraid she'd be judged. But that second year, she spent a lot of it.

After that time, Mama had money and she could do what she wanted to do and buy things she saw other mamas buy. She seemed happy.

For the first time in my life, I saw happiness in Mama's face.

Mama was free.

Chapter 20
Reaching for Raul

Out of all my brothers and sisters I was closest to Raul. He was the one who protected me the most. When I was in trouble, which was most of the time, and crying, which was much of the time, Raul would pat me on the back to calm me down and say, "Think about what you did, Leticia, what you said to Papa. You know, maybe he's right, maybe you're right, but it's not for us to set him back."

After sixth grade, Raul was pulled out of school so he could work in the fields with Papa and help bring money to the family. At sixteen, I think it was, he moved to the United States, met an Anglo woman in Napa, and worked in the vineyards there, planting seeds and picking grapes. He had children and grandchildren and lived a good life there.

Raul is the one who introduced me to Ramiro at the wedding in Vista Hermosa. Raul is the one who pointed him out.

"Look at that guy. Don't you think he's perfect for you?"

"No," I said because I was in love with Salvador who I was supposed to marry.

"Leticia, think about it. You don't have a house. You go back and forth between our house and our sister's house. You're already twenty. It's time."

Raul was a funny guy. He told jokes a lot, even as he was in the hospital with cancer. He would ask to see lady nurses because he was tired of seeing so many doctors and nurses that were men. I remember once when he was about to have surgery, he said to the doctor, "I don't care where you cut me, but never cut my butt! Cut here and here, but NOT THERE!"

Raul was popular. During the time he and his family lived in St. Helena, his house was full of friends. Every weekend he was entertaining them. He was the fun party guy and everyone wanted to be around him. Raul was so popular that when he was in the hospital and there were so many people in his room one doctor thought he was someone famous.

For fifteen years, Raul suffered from cancer, ever since he was twenty-four; he was living in Napa then. It started in his spine and then moved to different parts of his body. In those fifteen years, he had had thirteen surgeries.

The hardest part for Raul in the hospital was seeing the kids. He had his chemo treatments in the same room as they had theirs. He cried sometimes and then would say out loud, "God, why these children? They didn't do anything wrong. They don't even know this world. Why do you do this? Why are they in this room? I know how hard these treatments are. Why do these children suffer?"

Before Raul died we talked about our family, and Papa.

"Leticia, don't you think Papa was a good father to us?"

"No, Raul, he taught us the wrong way. He didn't show us a nice side, didn't show us or tell us that he loved us."

"Yes, I know."

But I had had that opportunity to spend time with Papa before he passed away and ask him all those questions, like why he was so hard on us, why he was so hard on me.

"At the end of his life, Raul, I told Papa I loved him. He told me he loved me too."

"I wish I had done that, to find out things. But you know Leticia, since I'm a man I don't ask those questions."

I told Raul that just because he was raised that way with Papa it didn't mean he couldn't express love to *his* children. Maybe it was time to tell them how he felt.

So he did.

I talked to Raul for two hours during the last day of his life. He told me what a good guy Ramiro was and how I needed to take care of him. He also told me how I shouldn't be disappointed because he was dying.

"You need to be strong, Leticia, day by day. Don't give up easily. And don't be like Mama being so quiet. Speak up. But also, you need to respect Ramiro."

Later, when Ramiro came into the hospital room, Raul talked to him also, "I know Leticia's pushy sometimes and needs to change her behavior sometimes, but she's a good worker. She's a good woman."

Ramiro reassured Raul that he and I would be equal and he'd never leave me.

After Raul said goodbye to everyone, he told me to come close and hold his hand. "Stay close to me, Leticia."

He looked up at the ceiling and said out loud: "God, I'm ready for you now." Raul's hand still held mine, so tight that somebody had to open it to let my hand free. In less than a minute, he was gone.

Raul died in 1994 at the age of thirty-nine years old, in Napa, where I often visit his gravesite. It is the place I go and open up my heart. I bring him flowers and we talk. *I* talk. In my dreams, I reach for Raul, take his hand, the one I held at the hospital when he was dying, remembering what he said in those last hard days: "Learn about yourself, Leticia. Learn and discover more."

Chapter 21
College

My sisters were jealous of me when we got older, I think because Mama talked highly of me. She got to know some things I did, like get awards in my hometown, help people who were sick, organize funerals, go to college. I was the one who didn't allow my husband to control me.

In our culture, you don't know anything different than that you need to obey your husband and do whatever he wants. I mean, it took me fifteen years before I went to college, no, maybe twenty. I finally went at forty-three years old. I figured Ramiro would get used to me getting an education. But he never did.

"You didn't marry me to go to college," he said. "You married me to have children and to make food and clean the house."

"Oh! So you are a macho Mexican man! I thought I married a man who lives in the United States and had changed."

Every time I had exams I had to study after Ramiro went to bed. I hid in a closet with my books and papers. I knew I needed to be responsible for Ramiro, but I needed to be responsible for my classes too.

After Ramiro would fall asleep, I'd pretend to fall asleep, and then soon after I'd get out of bed and walk to the closet. Once inside, I turned on a small light, sat down on the carpet, and leaned against one of the walls where I propped up a pillow. I would have studied downstairs, but we have an alarm, so if I walked downstairs Ramiro would have heard the alarm and asked me, "What are you doing," or "Where are you going?"

It was a big closet where I studied, the walk-in kind, filled with clothes, shoes, and a basket of dirty clothes, but I had room. Still, the light wasn't good and I was sitting on the floor. I'd study from around ten or eleven at night to two or three in the morning.

At the beginning of those years, I kept asking, *Why do I have to do this every night?* It seemed crazy. This was for seven years of my life.

Ramiro was angry with me throughout that time, repeating the same thing, "Stop going to college," and really, there were times I did want to stop; it would have been so much easier. But then, each morning I'd get up and say to myself, "No, you want to continue. Last night was hard, but today will be better." I knew if I stopped going to college I'd never go back.

The last two years were the hardest. Ramiro and I argued most of the time. Once, he didn't talk to me for three months. And then he threatened divorce.

Three weeks before I graduated, Ramiro said it again, "We are getting a divorce *now*. Right now."

"OK, Ramiro, if that's what you want, we'll do it. Are you going to get a lawyer, or am I? Because I'm tired of hearing this all the time. No matter what you think, I am not going to stop doing what I'm doing."

Ramiro never could accept that with a college degree I could make more money. I kept telling him it was my time to help; he had supported our family all those years.

After I graduated and Ramiro saw how my business improved, how respected I was, he apologized, telling me how sorry he was for what he did to me all those years. But how does a person make hard times like that disappear, act like they never happened. It was all inside of me, those seven years. And it still hurts.

Chapter 22
Interview with Mama

In April 2012, I interviewed my mama, Maria Gonzalez Garcia, who was ninety years old at the time—I was fifty-five—in Vista Hermosa. I sat on the edge of her bed, she sat on a chair opposite me, and I asked her questions in Spanish. Mama died on December 22, 2016.

"I was born in Unión de Guadalupe," Mama began. My father's name was Pancho Gonzalez, my mother's Luisa Villa. My mother was always affectionate with me, my father more detached. I had two brothers, Trinidad and Manuel.

We grew up in a small town, only twenty to thirty houses. The town was made up of a big ranch that always smelled like cows and chickens. I never had any kind of education, but I was happy in my childhood. When I was seven or eight, we moved to San Sebastian, but I wasn't happy there like I was at the ranch town.

After my grandparents died, my father, my aunt, and my uncle took me away from my mother because she was too sick to take care of me. It was a sad time.

I met your father at a church; he was painting there. We used to hide from our parents because they would get mad if they saw us together. José moved to Guadalajara to work but he would come to see me once a month.

We were fifteen when we got married. We were married one year from fifty years. At our wedding, I wore a long white dress and we had music and ate stuffed loin, rice, and fruit. It was a wonderful big party.

At seventeen I had my first child; all my children were born at home except for Ruben and Agueda. With them, I was sick with a high temperature and they had to transfer me to the hospital. All the others were born at home with the help of Doña Felix.

When I got to five children I didn't want anymore, but they kept coming and coming. I remember thinking, *There are already fifteen!* We couldn't take anything to stop having children then. They used to say it was a sin. We never talked about birth control. We never talked about menses.

All day long I cleaned the house because there were so many of you. On the side, I sold chickens to make a little money. I wanted my children, even daughters, to go to school, but your papa said girls didn't need to go because they'd be supported by their husbands. Women didn't support men. Women are for getting married, he said, being in the kitchen and having children. I stayed inside the house doing domestic chores—ironing, washing clothes, cooking, making tortillas. I didn't go outside or anything.

These days, women don't wash clothes, iron, and make tortillas. They are everywhere, not always at home. But I still think women should be at home. Home is a child's first school. Everything you say at home, they take in. But school is good. When the boys went to school in Tamazula, they learned to weld, make doors, use a lathe. I didn't want them to only work in the fields.

At eighty, I learned to read and write. I read government papers. I wrote a letter.

My strength comes from my children and from their helping me. And my religion. Religion gave me the strength to pray to God to help me with all of you. Your papa never went to church, I don't know why. He didn't have a religion.

There was that difficult time your papa started drinking a lot. He was going out with another woman; he even brought her to our house. How do I tell you about such a thing, how sad it was.

As for you, Leticia, you were a mischievous little girl. You were different, stubborn. I don't know why you are like that.

When you were nine or ten, you worked at the ranch for Don Miguel and Doña Josephina Cortez, helping with getting the groceries, cleaning their house, prepping food. You would come home dirty, and I would give you a bath and wash your clothes. You would cry and cry.

You didn't like to study and you didn't like sewing. You'd ask for the fabric to make tablecloths, but you never wanted to make them. Your sisters and I made all the tablecloths and servilletas for the tortillas, to make money for food.

You used to go roving about, wandering around town with your friend Felix, or you would dance; you loved to dance. Your papa would say, 'That girl is only good for dancing; she doesn't want to learn anything else.' We begged you to study, but you only studied when you went to America where you earned your degrees. I think you wanted to climb up by yourself.

Those times you came home from the United States and your sisters were lying around the house, you'd say, 'Come on! It's time to get up and start washing dishes and clean the house.' You always liked things fast. They used to call you "El Ventarron," a strong gust of wind. I saw how hard you worked.

Now women are worth the same as men. They work the same and they know more. And they have two or three children because times are difficult now, and, if there is no work for both parents it's hard. But, if both are working they can say, 'I will buy this and you will buy that.' These days it's equality.

Chapter 23
Mama's Last Words

She didn't want us crying; she was like Papa that way. "I don't want to see nobody crying. If you want to cry, go outside the room. Nobody is dying here. I'm just going through a difficult time."

She was in a lot of pain those last days, not eating, not talking much until she talked all the time. Even though she denied she was dying, it was clear she wanted to say what was on her mind.

"Leticia, this is the time I need to talk to you."

"Yes, Mama."

"I want you to be in charge of my will."

"Oh Mama, all the sisters will be angry with me. I don't think that's a good idea."

"No, Leticia, I want you to do that."

"Why do you trust me, to give me that job?"

"Because you never let me down. I don't even know why you are so different from all your brothers and sisters, but you have always helped me. Going to the United States, you helped me get a flight. You gave me my first birthday party when I was seventy years old. I will never forget that party. Remember those presents and how I said, 'Are all those for me?' I go through those pictures that give me such happy memories."

"When you were fifteen years old, working in the fields in Sacramento, you sent me checks to help with things here. You helped with the house, keeping it the way Papa liked to keep it. If something needed to be done, you'd do it. You wouldn't hesitate to change your clothes and start painting the walls. I never said thank you for all those things you did because we are not supposed to thank our children. This is why I'm giving you the job."

When Mama was in the hospital, I visited her for long periods of time. My sisters and brothers visited too, but they would talk and gossip and use their cell phones. What is the quality of time they give to Mama when she was so ill? I saw how they dropped by, gave her a kiss, asked, "Comó estás, Mama?" Then thirty minutes they'd be gone.

You ever lie down with your mama? You ever clean her body, even after she went pee and poo? You ever feed her because she can't use a spoon? You ever tell the hospital they need to change the sheets because they're dirty?

"You know what?" I said to my sisters and brothers, "This is your mama, and one day you're going to be just like this."

It took me two days to say yes to Mama, to be in charge of her will.

"There is something else I'd like to talk to you about," she said. "Agueda."

"Agueda?"

"Yes, Leticia, I want you to change her."

"Change her?"

"You need to teach her the way you are with your husband. The way you're independent. She works two jobs, selling jewelry, selling shoes at home. Her husband doesn't do anything to improve anything. It's been twelve, thirteen years since they had a relationship. He doesn't let her do anything or go anywhere without him. I don't want Agueda to be the way I was in my marriage."

I was mad at Agueda for many years because I thought she was taking advantage of Mama, taking her money for herself and her husband. But after Mama passed I think it was Agueda who had the hardest time. She missed Mama a lot, and not just because of money. They had become good friends.

After Mama died, she had the typical funeral that they held in our town. Before the funeral, the body remains at the house, or more like outside the house in a courtyard or breezeway. They fix up the body so it looks nice as people stop by. Mama had chosen her own dress to be worn at the funeral, pink and ivory. As part of her instructions, she said, "I don't want my mouth open." After so many days, a dead body's mouth opens up, so you need to put something in there so it stays closed. She wanted to be perfect that day.

Two days later, a limo drives the body to the church, and everybody walks behind the car like a procession in the streets. The church isn't far from Mama's house, so it was a short walk.

At the church, they held a mass, a Catholic mass of course, where the casket is open, so if someone wanted to talk to Mama or touch her or say goodbye they could. I was in the pews holding two of my sisters' hands.

After we got back to the house after mass, that's the time all the trouble started.

We had just walked into the main room and the will came up, and two of my sisters started yelling at me.

"Why did Mama choose *you*, Leticia? Why do *you* always make the decisions?"

"I didn't make the decision. Mama did! And really, who was the person who gave you money, and Mama, money? Who was worried about Mama when she needed medications? Who paid for Mama to visit the United States? When Papa passed away, who paid for his funeral? Today is Mama's funeral! And you want to argue?"

Two weeks after Mama passed, I came back to Vista Hermosa to give the papers to my sisters and brothers. And to distribute the money. I gave my own money to a sister who needed it. Eva gave her money to another sister who needed it. But still, most sisters and brothers were angry with me.

It was a horrible time, my mama's death, except for the three days and three nights I spent with her at the hospital. I put makeup on her and perfume because Mama always liked to look nice.

"Do you have a mirror so I can see my face? How do I look?"

Mama didn't recognize me at first, that time I came to see her in the hospital from the United States. And then she did. At the moment she remembered me, she patted the space next to her, as if to say, "There is your place, child." That was my signal to lie down next to Mama, which I often did.

"Just remember, Leticia, you have a good husband. Take care of him because you won't find anyone else. He helps you more than any other man in a marriage. And one more thing. I want you to bring our family together."

That's the promise I made to Mama.

"Yes, Mama, we will call each other and see each other."

"You are different from your brothers and sisters, Leticia."

"Yes, Mama, I know."

I called Agueda from California and asked if she'd buy sunflowers to put on Mama's grave. Bright yellow, with all those petals circling the center.

Today

Chapter 24
Jesus in a Glass House,
Guadalupe in Every House

When I talked to Mama at the end of her life, I asked her about Papa and the way he treated her. That was an unusual thing to do, to talk to your mama or papa about their private business. But I wanted to know. I always wanted to know.

"Why didn't you say nothing to Papa when he was screaming at you, when he hit you, when he was cheating on you?"

"Look at the years I was living, Leticia," Mama said. "Look at the time. You say something to your husband, they just go and find someone else. How many children did I have by then? Ten? Twelve? How was I going to say something to your papa?"

"Yes, Mama, but what about Eliaser? She's the same age as you. She stood up for herself."

"But I didn't have the courage to do that. I wasn't conditioned to do something like that. My mama taught me to behave, to help children, to feed my husband. After I came to the United States and saw how you lived and then went back home, I knew it was too late for me."

"You never tried, Mama? You never said nothing? He brought that lady, right into your home!"

Papa used to dance in the streets to the mariachi music and drink tequila with women. Everybody did that. That was normal. One time he brought a woman to their house.

My sisters, too, they had problems with their husbands.

When I was seven or eight, I saw one of my sister's husband's drinking and my sister with bruises because he had opened the car door and pushed her out. She came to our house and I was thinking, *You don't want to bring those problems here*. I told her, "If our Papa comes home early from work and finds you in the house, Mama will get in trouble. You can't stay here, you know what will happen. Papa will hit Mama because she is not doing her job. She is not supposed to let her children do whatever they want to do."

I remember the time Papa got mad at Mama for not ironing his handkerchief, the red bandana he used to wipe his nose with. He hit her for not ironing it, and then he hit me for speaking up for Mama. I knew everything that was going to happen if we didn't do what Papa always told us to do.

I said what I felt, which was why I was in trouble all the time, which was why Papa wondered why I wasn't like my sisters. Papa said I should never talk back, that I needed to agree with everything he said.

"Si, Papa."

But it wasn't me.

Papa didn't like me to look into his eyes when I got into trouble, but I always did. Except for that one time.

That one time, the school principal came to our house because Papa had pulled me out of class, only three months before I graduated from 6th grade. He had shown up at

100

school early one day. I was dressed in my blue and white volleyball uniform, which he didn't approve of because he didn't believe girls should wear shorts.

"This is the last day you're going to school!"

I was crying and trying to talk to him.

"You don't have the right to tell me I can't play sports because you think sports are only for boys and not for girls!"

That was the worst hit I ever had with his belt. I looked down at the floor instead of his eyes like I usually did, to say I was sorry, but I wasn't. Sorry.

Those times Papa was like that I prayed to Our Lady Guadalupe—*Where are you, Guadalupe? Where are you to help Mama and to help me when I'm sad and crying?*

In the middle of our town, we have four life-sized statues of followers of Jesus, from the Bible, lit at night in glass houses, see-through exhibits. The glass houses sit in the middle of the road, dividing it into two; one road skirts the glass house on its right, the other road skirts the glass house on its left. Below the statues, on an easel, is a framed picture of Jesus in his white robe.

What is a glass house but a building separating one thing from another?

Guadalupe, she's not in a glass house. She's in our homes, our church, embossed in gold charms hung around our necks. She's represented in paintings, in photographs, in statues. At the altar of our church, she's the one who's in the center, not Jesus. In a beautiful artwork of stained glass, a gold frame surrounding her, white and red roses intertwined around the frame, she stands with her hands, palm to palm in prayer, the mother of all mothers, the one to care for us, to love us. Below her picture, also in stained glass, reads the words:

NO ESTOY YO AQUI QUE SOY TU MADRE

Am I Not Here, Me That Is Your Mother.

In Mama's house, a small painting of Guadalupe greets every family member, friend, and visitor, in the entryway of her home. Inside her house, she's there again, in every room: "Cry to me, and of those who seek and place their trust in me."

But where was Guadalupe when *I* was weeping? When Papa hit Mama, when Papa hit me, when Papa stood on the side as Mama raised fifteen children? When Papa was with other women? Is Guadalupe not a woman herself? Does she not know how it feels to be treated like we don't matter? Is she not the matriarch of all matriarchs?

Guadalupe tells us to trust her, and I do, even with all my unanswered prayers, I do…trust her. I pray to her in the morning and light candles for her at night. I still believe in her. Still. And yet, if I could have a little private talk with the Virgin Mary, I know what I'd ask.

Guadalupe, how does it feel to be a woman in a man's world?

And I wonder what'd she say.

Chapter 25
Jealous

Maybe because I'm fifteen years younger. Maybe because I like to look nice. Maybe because I dress up sometimes. Maybe because I have a nice figure. Maybe because I have a successful business. Maybe these are the reasons Ramiro is jealous, even after all this time.

"A wife isn't supposed to make money for the family," Ramiro tells me. "While I worked at the lumber mill, I was the one making the money. Now you're making the money."

He was jealous that I made money. Jealous that I dressed up nicely. Jealous that I had friends I wanted to go out with.

Ramiro believed that during my college years I was going to pick up younger men. But I was the same age as the teachers, not the students. I was older. I was married. To Ramiro.

Or maybe he's jealous because his first wife found someone else.

Jealousy. It's all over our culture.

I know a young woman, twenty-four years old, who went to a dance in Reno. Because some man looked at her, her husband hit him.

A good friend of mine, here in America, the same age as me, has been married more than thirty years; she has no life of her own. Her husband doesn't want her to do anything without him. One time, she and I, just the two of us, went to a restaurant to have a drink and eat dinner. Every two minutes she asked me what time it was. Her husband didn't know we were at a restaurant. She lied and told him something else.

After my friend got home, her husband got so mad he left the house...for three days! Their daughter called him, worried.

"When are you coming back, Papa?"

"I'm not coming back, I'm angry with your mama."

It was my son's birthday after those three days, and so he finally showed up, at my son's party.

"Do you want something to eat?" my friend said, running to her husband, "Here, I'll make you a plate. What would you like?"

"No, I don't want nothing!" he said. Just like that.

I told my friend if her husband wanted a plate of food he could walk over and get it. He can serve himself, you know.

I'm scared for my friend because I can talk to her, give her suggestions for how to get help, but I cannot do everything for her.

Another woman I know, nineteen, married with one child, her husband verbally and physically abuses her, and this thing that he does, it's hard to even talk about it.

This husband doesn't want her to work, but she found a job, so he allowed her to go out; he knew they needed money. But, this unbelievable thing he does.

Every time she comes home from work—she was crying when she told me this—her husband needs to smell her private area to be sure she didn't do anything with another guy.

"Every day when I come home, he does that."

One day she pushed him away, trying to be strong, telling him to stop.

"I'm not going to let you do that anymore. You need to trust me. If you don't trust me, I'll stop working."

While she has her periods they have sex, even though she doesn't want to.

"You need to respect your body," I told her. "You need to put your feet on the floor and say how you feel. You need to get help because this is something too big for you."

She doesn't have any family in the United States. She is alone, and while she wants to make things better, she says that her husband drinks, and it's impossible to approach him.

So many people I know in our small town in the United States that have these problems.

We grow up with fathers who tell us we can't get divorced and a religion that tells us we can't get a divorce. Our husbands follow our fathers and become the next man to tell us what we can and can't do. But our husbands are not our fathers, and we are not their young children.

When it's like this, I ask myself, *How can we be ourselves?*

Chapter 26
Small Steps

"This is a really nice dress. Here, try it on."

"But my husband needs to come and see if it's okay."

"Agueda, *I'm* buying you the dress," I tell my sister. "You don't have to show it to your husband. If you like it, I'll buy it. Go ahead, try it on."

"If I don't show it to him, he won't let me wear it."

"Really, it's not a problem. I want to buy it for you. After all, it's for my husband's birthday party."

"No, I can't. I just can't."

This younger sister, she doesn't know what's inside her.

My older sister, Concha, never asks permission for anything. She was the one who made Papa go to the church when I got married. Concha has a mind of her own. She does what she wants to do. Her life is really something.

But my brothers treat their wives the same as Papa. And their wives don't do nothing about it. They ask their husbands anytime they want to do something. They ask permission. To go somewhere. To buy something. I believe their wives are going to die like that.

Those times I go out with friends, I tell my husband ahead of time I'm going. Most times I'm back home for dinner; I'm just having a glass of wine for an hour or so. Sometimes I go out for dinner, and if I do I tell my husband "Here is your dinner. I love you, I'll be back soon." I tell my friends this and encourage them to start doing things on their own. Small. Step by step.

"Never expect your husband to say he's happy you're doing things on your own," I told one friend. "You will never hear that. Be on your own to be on your own."

I am not liked, even hated by some men in my community. They don't want me to be friends with their wives.

"What are you telling her?" they'll ask me.

"I'm teaching your wife about nutrition for your family," or "I'm helping your wife learn English."

And these are true.

But I also talk to these women, young and old, and tell them *Tomorrow could be so much different than today*.

You could drive. You could go to college. You could handle your own money, not your husband who gives you an allowance every week, even as you bring money home. You could go out with friends, travel, do things you want to do, do things without your husband.

Many women stay home because they don't know what is inside them. They don't think about tomorrow. They have no dreams. No plans.

How many women want to do something? How many want to *be* somebody other than who they've been all their lives?

I know women who don't know who to talk to; they don't know where to go; they don't have a place.

But there is always a place.

A place to start.

Tomorrow

Chapter 27
Ramiro Changing

It started three months ago. In Colima. We had finished building our house there, in Mexico, and had started going to Colima every couple of months. Just Ramiro and me. But when we went there, he acted differently than in California. Like the Mexican macho man. Again. Why?

"Why do you change in Mexico?" I asked him. "*You* have to drive. *You* have to have the money. I can't go anywhere without you."

I was just thinking the other day that maybe I'll buy my own car so I can drive to wherever I want to drive to. I'll ask Ramiro, "Would you like to come with me or stay at home?"

In Colima, Ramiro even bought some exercise equipment for our house so I wouldn't go to the gym in town.

"You know, Leticia, I know you're not happy here. If you want to get a divorce, we can do that. Split the money and that's that."

We had talked about divorce so many times before; this wasn't anything new.

"OK, if that's what you want, let's do it."

At this stage in my life, I wasn't about to stay in Mexico only to be in the house all day with no independence. I wasn't sure Ramiro was serious this time, but if this was how it was going to be I wanted out too.

So, I called my son in California.

"Could you give me that lawyer's phone number because I need to talk to him."

In front of Ramiro, I called the lawyer and asked for his advice on how to get started. I don't know if Ramiro was serious about getting a divorce, but at this point, *I* was.

"Be smart, Leticia," the lawyer said, "as I know you are. Yes, I can help you."

We talked some more and I received more details on the process.

It took two weeks for Ramiro to talk to me, he was so mad.

After we returned to California from Colima, Ramiro started to change. "What can I do for you? What do you want me to cook? Do you want to go someplace this weekend?"

Is this my husband? I thought.

On Valentine's Day, Ramiro bought me flowers and arranged a dinner reservation at a restaurant in town. He never did that. Every morning, now, he gives me a kiss. He never did that either. There's no, "Where are you going? Why are you going?" "Who are you going with?" There's no "You can't go out."

Ramiro has changed one hundred percent. It is like a new marriage, a new beginning.

I feel like this change is Ramiro thinking *I never thought Leticia would follow through on a divorce.* And when I made it clear I would, he didn't want to do it after all, not after thirty-nine years of marriage.

But I know if we go back to how it was, I am not a person in my sixties to be treated like that.

Yet, I'm not completely there.

I'm not one-hundred percent independent.

But I'm closer than I've ever been.

Chapter 28
Skin Deep

It was the best of the best. Seventy family members—my sisters, cousins, nieces, and brothers-in-law. We had a mariachi band, and then another band played until ten at night. We danced from the beginning to the end. It was my sixty-second birthday.

Everything was perfect at the beautiful resort and the room we rented in Colima. Everybody was singing, everybody happy. My friend Martha sang one of Mama's favorites with the mariachi band, a song that said something about 'forget the past.'

Friends from Los Angeles came, and Mexico, my sister from Veracruz, others from Guadalajara, Colima, and Vista Hermosa. Everybody brought their families, and after the party they drank and danced and sang all night back at their motel.

We had appetizers at the party and a big cake. The tables had tablecloths down to the floor with large flower arrangements set in the center of each table. Everything was real dishes, no paper plates.

It was the first time everyone got along, all my sisters and me. The fight we had at Mama's funeral was over. We were getting too old to act like that.

But then there was Alejandra. The last one to make peace.

After my birthday party in Colima, I went to *her* birthday party in Napa. Her daughter invited me because Alejandra and I hadn't talked in two years. Ever since we were kids, she was angry with me, mostly when I told her I didn't like the way her husband was treating her. I told her that as a child.

During Mama's time in the hospital those last days, Alejandra and I started to argue again, but I didn't want Mama to see that. I told her, "If you want to talk to me, we need to go outside the room. I don't want Mama to hear that garbage."

"Leticia, I am angry with you because you are the more beautiful sister. You always dress nicely and wear high heels. You are free from your husband."

Free from my husband? This wasn't the discussion we needed to have right then.

"That's what you have against me? I dress nicely, and am independent? How much does that hurt you inside? How much does that hurt me? I invited everyone to my birthday party in Colima and everybody came except you and Eva who was sick. You said you needed to save money because you needed it for your celebration for your husband in November in Mexico. I'm going to go to *your* party, and I need to save money too. I work hard every day to support my family."

When I went to Napa to celebrate Alejandra's birthday, I brought her flowers and wrote a long note on her birthday card to try to get her to understand that as sisters, as family, we needed to get along.

I had always wondered why this sister seemed sad all the time, quiet. But I finally learned her sadness revolved around her skin color. She had the darkest skin a Mexican could have; she was the darkest one in our family. As she got older, she did a cleanup of her face, a laser procedure. Now she's kind of white. I don't know why she did that, but maybe she wasn't strong enough to accept the color of her skin. Alejandra felt like she wasn't her mother's daughter. She was feeling down all the time.

I understood how she felt all alone with a different colored skin, but I had my own problems.

"How do you think *I* felt that time I found out my name wasn't Leticia?"

As a requirement for graduating from sixth grade I needed my birth certificate. We went to the registration office in town, but they said, "There's no Leticia registered here." It turned out my real name is Maria Bertha Alicia. In the United States, I brought my new name with me, but I wasn't going to give up Leticia; that's who I always was.

When I discovered my name was different, Mama said, "I got so many children and there are so many daughters, I forgot your name."

"How would you feel, Alejandra? You think I'm going to be sad all my life because of that?"

But a funny thing happened. Ramiro learned my real name and started laughing. "Well, Bertha Alicia, my ex-wife's name is Bertha Alicia."

"Well, honey," I said to Ramiro, "You're certainly never going to call me that!"

Alejandra didn't know my story, and it might not have seemed a big deal. But it was to me, just as her dark skin was to her. Not only did Mama forget my name, she told me my birthday was March 9th, instead of March 28th.

"You are so different from the others, Leticia, I don't even know you are my child," Mama said repeatedly. Alejandra and I both felt less of a person because of these things.

Things got right between us, though. I turned sixty-two and a few weeks later Alejandra turned seventy and we were talking again...after most of our lives were behind us.

Epilogue
Tomatoes

I was standing in the tomato section at the grocery store, looking them over carefully because I wanted to pick the best ones. I put the tomatoes into a plastic bag, but then I noticed this really tall guy staring at me. "Stupid Mexicans," he said.

I looked right into his eyes like I used to do with Papa. "You know what?" I said, "You are ignorant!" He thought I didn't understand English; he said that to me.

I left. And I left my bag of tomatoes. I wasn't scared he would do something; I just wanted to get away so he wouldn't say anything more. Nobody can hurt me like that.

People in my town in California ask me, "What is the best way to respond to comments like that?" I tell them…

"Stay firm."

"Look into their eyes."

"Say how you feel."

If you let people say harmful things to you, you are never going to know what it means to respect people and to have respect for yourself. If you let people step on you, do you think that's right? You are human. You are not wood. You are not a rock.

For me, when life is hard, when I am criticized for being a Mexican or because I'm a woman, or even worse, prevented from *doing things* because I'm a woman, like driving, getting an education, traveling, or being with friends, I get depressed. I don't sleep. I lose weight. I get mad. I get worried. I try to be a tough person, but sometimes it gets me right in here, in my heart. But tomorrow, I tell myself, I will think differently. If I don't do that, I will go down, down, down. And I don't want to go down that hill. I want to go up it.

Leticia Aguilar: Owner of Lety's Preschool and Immersion Program in Truckee, California. Board Member of several family organizations. Associate degrees in Early Childhood Education and Early Childhood Education Master Teacher. Recipient of awards from the Family Resource Center of Truckee, Soroptimist International of Truckee Donner, and Truckee Interclub. She lives in Truckee with her husband, and has two sons, one daughter, and three grandchildren.

Eve Quesnel: Co-editor of *The Biosphere and the Bioregion: Essential Writings of Peter Berg*, 2015, Routledge. Retired Sierra College English Instructor. She lives in Truckee with her husband and has one daughter and one grandchild.

Photographs by Wade Snider